To

Rachel

From

♡ Emily

To one of the most
kind hearted people
I know!

Broadstreet Publishing
Racine, WI 53403
Broadstreetpublishing.com

Bible Promises for Mothers
© 2014 by Broadstreet Publishing

ISBN 978-1-4245-4900-9

Compiled by Amy Stevens and Barbara Farmer
Cover design by Josh Lewandowski
Interior design by James Baker | www.jamesbakerdesign.com

Printed in China

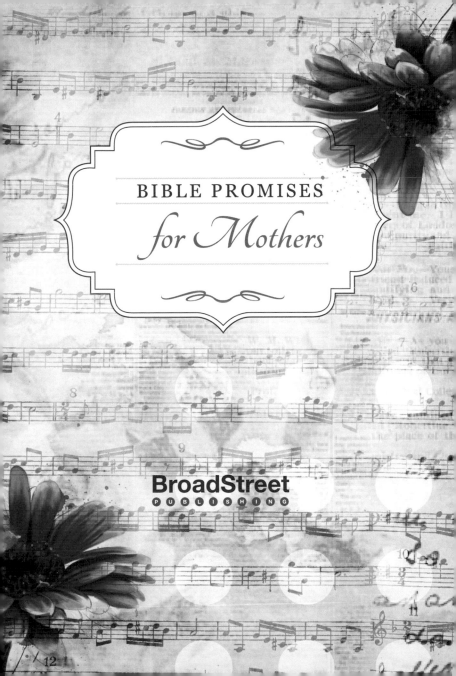

Contents

Alpha

GOD IS THE FIRST PLACE TO GO FOR ALL WE NEED.

"I am the Alpha and the Omega, the Beginning
and the End," says the Lord, "who is and who was
and who is to come, the Almighty."

REVELATION 1:8 NKJV

I fall to my knees and pray to the Father,
the Creator of everything in heaven and on earth.
I pray that from his glorious, unlimited resources
he will empower you with inner strength through
his Spirit. Then Christ will make his home
in your hearts as you trust in him.

EPHESIANS 3:14–17 NLT

My God will supply
all your needs according to
His riches in glory in Christ Jesus.

PHILIPPIANS 4:19 NASB

Lord, you have been our dwelling place
throughout all generations.
Before the mountains were born
or you brought forth the whole world,
from everlasting to everlasting you are God.

PSALM 90:1–2 NIV

Abandonment

The LORD your God is living among you.
He is a mighty savior.
He will take delight in you with gladness.
With his love, he will calm all your fears.
He will rejoice over you with joyful songs.

ZEPHANIAH 3:17 NLT

You, God, see the trouble of the afflicted;
you consider their grief and take it in hand.
The victims commit themselves to you;
you are the helper of the fatherless.

PSALM 10:14 NIV

Those who know the LORD trust him,
because he will not leave those who come to him.

PSALM 9:10 NCV

Not a single sparrow can fall to the
ground without your Father knowing it.
And the very hairs on your head are all numbered.
So don't be afraid; you are more valuable to God
than a whole flock of sparrows.

MATTHEW 10:29–31 NLT

Be strong and courageous. Do not be afraid or terrified
because of them, for the LORD your God goes with you;
he will never leave you nor forsake you.

DEUTERONOMY 31:6 NIV

God makes a home for the lonely;
He leads out the prisoners into prosperity.

PSALM 68:6 NASB

Abuse

LORD, you know the hopes of the helpless.
Surely you will hear their cries and comfort them.
You will bring justice to the orphans and the oppressed,
so mere people can no longer terrify them.

PSALM 10:17–18 NLT

The everlasting God is your place of safety,
and his arms will hold you up forever.

DEUTERONOMY 33:27 NCV

When you go through deep waters and great trouble,
I will be with you. When you go through rivers
of difficulty, you will not drown! When you walk through
the fire of oppression, you will not be burned up—
the flames will not consume you.

ISAIAH 43:2 TLB

The LORD is close to the brokenhearted
and saves those who are crushed in spirit.

PSALM 34:18 NIV

The spirit of the Lord GOD is upon me…
he has sent me to bring good news to the oppressed,
to bind up the brokenhearted,
to proclaim liberty to the captives,
and release to the prisoners…
to provide for those who mourn…
to give them a garland instead of ashes,
the oil of gladness instead of mourning,
the mantle of praise instead of a faint spirit.

ISAIAH 61:1, 3 NRSV

Acceptance

Our steps are made firm by the LORD,
when he delights in our way;
though we stumble, we shall not fall headlong,
for the LORD holds us by the hand.

PSALM 37:23–24 NRSV

Here I am! I stand at the door and knock. If anyone hears
my voice and opens the door, I will come in and
eat with that person, and they with me.

REVELATION 3:20 NIV

We have come to know and have believed the love which
God has for us. God is love, and the one who abides
in love abides in God, and God abides in him.
We love, because He first loved us.

1 JOHN 4:16, 19 NASB

I've redeemed you.

I've called your name. You're mine.

When you're in over your head, I'll be there with you.

When you're in rough waters, you will not go down.

When you're between a rock and a hard place,

it won't be a dead end—

Because I am GOD, your personal God,

The Holy of Israel, your Savior.

I paid a huge price for you...!

That's how much you mean to me!

That's how much I love you!

ISAIAH 43:1–4 MSG

Addiction

Show me the right path, O Lord;
point out the road for me to follow.
Lead me by your truth and teach me,
for you are the God who saves me.
All day long I put my hope in you.

PSALM 25:4–5 NLT

I am the light of the world. Whoever follows me will never
walk in darkness, but will have the light of life.

JOHN 8:12 NIV

I'll take the hand of those who don't know the way,
who can't see where they're going.
I'll be a personal guide to them,
directing them through unknown country.

ISAIAH 46:16 MSG

I would have you learn this great fact: that a life of doing right is the wisest life there is. If you live that kind of life, you'll not limp or stumble as you run. Carry out my instructions; don't forget them, for they will lead you to real living.

PROVERBS 4:11–13 TLB

The LORD is my shepherd, I shall not want.
He makes me lie down in green pastures;
he leads me beside still waters;
he restores my soul.
He leads me in right paths
for his name's sake.

PSALM 23:1–3 NRSV

Anger

Everyone should be quick to listen, slow to speak and slow to become angry, because human anger does not produce the righteousness that God desires.

JAMES 1:19–20 NIV

When you are praying, if you are angry with someone, forgive him so that your Father in heaven will also forgive your sins.

MARK 11:25 NCV

A gentle answer turns away wrath,
But a harsh word stirs up anger.

PROVERBS 15:1 NASB

Whoever is slow to anger has great understanding, but one who has a hasty temper exalts folly.

PROVERBS 14:29 NRSV

Brothers and sisters, whatever is true, whatever is noble,
whatever is right, whatever is pure, whatever is lovely,
whatever is admirable—if anything is excellent
or praiseworthy—think about such things.

PHILIPPIANS 4:8 NIV

Get rid of all bitterness, rage, anger, harsh words,
and slander, as well as all types of evil behavior. Instead, be
kind to each other, tenderhearted, forgiving one another,
just as God through Christ has forgiven you.

EPHESIANS 4:31–32 NLT

Refrain from anger and turn from wrath;
do not fret—it leads only to evil.

PSALM 37:8 NIV

Beauty

Don't be concerned about the outward beauty of
fancy hairstyles, expensive jewelry, or beautiful clothes.
You should clothe yourselves instead with the beauty that
comes from within, the unfading beauty of a gentle and
quiet spirit, which is so precious to God.

1 PETER 3:3–4 NLT

The LORD does not look at the things people look at.
People look at the outward appearance,
but the LORD looks at the heart.

1 SAMUEL 16:7 NIV

I will praise You, for I am fearfully and
wonderfully made; marvelous are Your works,
and that my soul knows very well.

PSALM 139:14 NKJV

Can any one of you by worrying add a single hour
to your life? And why do you worry about clothes?
See how the flowers of the field grow. They do not labor
or spin. Yet I tell you that not even Solomon in all his
splendor was dressed like one of these.

MATTHEW 6:27–29 NIV

The Lord is all I need.
He takes care of me.
My share in life has been pleasant;
my part has been beautiful.

PSALM 16:5–6 NCV

God has made everything beautiful in its time.

ECCLESIASTES 3:11 NIV

Blessings

Every good and perfect gift is from above,
coming down from the Father of the heavenly lights,
who does not change like shifting shadows.

JAMES 1:17 NIV

How blessed all those in whom you live,
whose lives become roads you travel;
They wind through lonesome valleys, come upon brooks,
discover cool springs and pools brimming with rain!

PSALM 84:5–6 MSG

Oh, taste and see that the LORD is good;
Blessed is the man who trusts in Him!

PSALM 34:8 NKJV

From his abundance we have all received
one gracious blessing after another.

JOHN 1:16 NLT

When you give a dinner or a supper,
do not ask...your relatives, nor rich neighbors,
lest they also invite you back, and you be repaid.
But...invite the poor, the maimed, the lame, the blind.
And you will be blessed.

LUKE 14:12–14 NKJV

The LORD bless you, and keep you;
The LORD make His face shine on you,
And be gracious to you;
The LORD lift up His countenance on you,
And give you peace.

NUMBERS 6:24–26 NASB

May the LORD richly bless
both you and your children.

PSALM 115:14 NLT

Caring

Bear one another's burdens, and in this way
you will fulfill the law of Christ.

GALATIANS 6:2 NRSV

If anyone has material possessions and sees a brother or
sister in need but has no pity on them, how can the love of
God be in that person? Dear children, let us not love with
words or speech but with actions and in truth.

1 JOHN 3:17–18 NIV

Do not *merely* look out for your own personal interests,
but also for the interests of others.

PHILIPPIANS 2:4 NASB

I was hungry and you gave me something to eat,
I was thirsty and you gave me something to drink, I was a
stranger and you invited me in, I needed clothes and you
clothed me, I was sick and you looked after me,
I was in prison and you came to visit me....
Whatever you did for one of the least of these brothers
and sisters of mine, you did for me.

MATTHEW 25:35–36, 40 NIV

Pure and genuine religion in the sight of God the Father
means caring for orphans and widows in their distress.

JAMES 1:27 NLT

Children

Direct your children onto the right path,
and when they are older, they will not leave it.

PROVERBS 22:6 NLT

These words which I command you today
shall be in your heart. You shall teach them diligently
to your children, and shall talk of them when you
sit in your house, when you walk by the way,
when you lie down, and when you rise up.

DEUTERONOMY 6:6–7 NKJV

Let the little children come to Me,
and do not forbid them;
for of such is the kingdom of heaven.

MATTHEW 19:14 NKJV

A refusal to correct is a refusal to love;
love your children by disciplining them.

PROVERBS 13:24 MSG

Any of you who welcomes a little child like this because
you are mine, is welcoming me.... Don't look down upon
a single one of these little children. For I tell you that in
heaven their angels have constant access to my Father.

MATTHEW 18:5, 10 TLB

Children are a gift from the LORD;
they are a reward from him.

PSALM 127:3 NLT

I have no greater joy than to hear that my children
are walking in the truth.

3 JOHN 1:4 NIV

Compassion

The Lord longs to be gracious to you;
therefore he will rise up to show you compassion.
For the Lord is a God of justice.
Blessed are all who wait for him!

Isaiah 30:18 NIV

Be gracious to me, O God,
according to Your lovingkindness;
According to the greatness of Your compassion
blot out my transgressions.

Psalm 51:1 NASB

Remember, O Lord, your compassion and unfailing love,
which you have shown from long ages past.

Psalm 25:6 NLT

What happens when we live God's way? He brings gifts
into our lives, much the same way that fruit appears
in an orchard—things like affection for others,
exuberance about life, serenity. We develop a willingness to
stick with things, a sense of compassion in the heart, and a
conviction that a basic holiness permeates things
and people. We find ourselves involved in
loyal commitments, not needing to force our way in life,
able to marshal and direct our energies wisely.

GALATIANS 5:22–23 MSG

Praise be to the God and Father of our Lord Jesus Christ,
the Father of compassion and the God of all comfort.

2 CORINTHIANS 1:3 NIV

Contentment

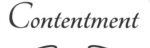

You're blessed when you're content with just who you are—
no more, no less. That's the moment you find yourselves
proud owners of everything that can't be bought.

MATTHEW 5:5 MSG

I know what it is to be in need,
and I know what it is to have plenty.
I have learned the secret of being content in any
and every situation, whether well fed or hungry,
whether living in plenty or in want.
I can do all this through him
who gives me strength.

PHILIPPIANS 4:12–13 NIV

If God cares so wonderfully for wildflowers that are here today and thrown into the fire tomorrow, he will certainly care for you. Why do you have so little faith? So don't worry about these things, saying, "What will we eat? What will we drink? What will we wear?" These things dominate the thoughts of unbelievers, but your heavenly Father already knows all your needs. Seek the Kingdom of God above all else, and live righteously, and he will give you everything you need.

MATTHEW 6:30–33 NLT

If you're content to simply be yourself, your life will count for plenty.

MATTHEW 23:11 MSG

Confidence

This is the confidence that we have in Him, that if we
ask anything according to His will, He hears us. And if we
know that He hears us, whatever we ask, we know that we
have the petitions that we have asked of Him.

1 JOHN 5:14–15 NKJV

I am confident of this very thing, that He who began a good
work in you will perfect it until the day of Christ Jesus.

PHILIPPIANS 1:6 NASB

Let us then approach God's throne of grace
with confidence, so that we may receive mercy and find
grace to help us in our time of need.

HEBREWS 4:16 NIV

I can do everything through Christ,
who gives me strength.

PHILIPPIANS 4:13 NLT

Be my rock of refuge,
to which I can always go;
give the command to save me,
for you are my rock and my fortress....
You have been my hope, Sovereign LORD,
my confidence since my youth.

PSALM 71:3, 5 NIV

The LORD will be your confidence,
And will keep your foot from being caught.

PROVERBS 3:26 NKJV

Courage

Be strong in the Lord and in his mighty power.
Put on the full armor of God, so that you can take
your stand against the devil's schemes.

EPHESIANS 6:10–11 NIV

Even though I walk
through the darkest valley,
I will fear no evil,
for you are with me;
your rod and your staff,
they comfort me.

PSALM 23:4 NIV

May He give you the power to accomplish all the good
things your faith prompts you to do.

2 THESSALONIANS 1:11 NLT

Keep alert, stand firm in your faith, be courageous,
be strong. Let all that you do be done in love.

1 CORINTHIANS 16:13–14 NRSV

Whenever I am afraid,
I will trust in You.
In God (I will praise His word),
In God I have put my trust;
I will not fear.

PSALM 56:3–4 NKJV

Be strong and courageous; do not be frightened
or dismayed, for the LORD your God
is with you wherever you go.

JOSHUA 1:9 NRSV

Depression

I keep asking that the God of our Lord Jesus Christ,
the glorious Father, may give you the Spirit of wisdom
and revelation, so that you may know him better. I pray
that the eyes of your heart may be enlightened in order
that you may know the hope to which he has called you,
the riches of his glorious inheritance in his holy people,
and his incomparably great power for us who believe.

EPHESIANS 1:17–19 NIV

I will give them a crown to replace their ashes,
and the oil of gladness to replace their sorrow,
and clothes of praise to replace their spirit of sadness.

ISAIAH 61:3 NCV

In all these things we are more than conquerors through him who loved us. For I am convinced that neither death nor life, neither angels nor demons, neither the present nor the future, nor any powers, neither height nor depth, nor anything else in all creation, will be able to separate us from the love of God that is in Christ Jesus our Lord.

ROMANS 8:37–39 NIV

God remembered us when we were down....
Takes care of everyone in time of need.
His love never quits.

PSALM 136:23, 25 MSG

Encouragement

Those who hope in the LORD
will renew their strength.
They will soar on wings like eagles;
they will run and not grow weary,
they will walk and not be faint.

ISAIAH 40:31 NIV

No eye has seen, no ear has heard, and no mind
has imagined what God has prepared
for those who love him.

1 CORINTHIANS 2:9 NLT

Everything that was written in the past was written to teach
us, so that through the endurance taught in the Scriptures
and the encouragement they provide we might have hope.

ROMANS 15:4 NIV

May our Lord Jesus Christ himself and God our Father...
encourage your hearts and strengthen you in every good
deed and word.

2 THESSALONIANS 2:16–17 NIV

Be quick to give a meal to the hungry, a bed to the
homeless—cheerfully. Be generous with the different things
God gave you, passing them around so all get in on it:
if words, let it be God's words; if help, let it be
God's hearty help. That way, God's bright presence
will be evident in everything.

1 PETER 4:9–11 MSG

Let everything you say be good and helpful, so that your
words will be an encouragement to those who hear them.

EPHESIANS 4:29 NLT

Enthusiasm

Work with enthusiasm, as though you were working for the Lord rather than for people. Remember that the Lord will reward each one of us for the good we do.

EPHESIANS 6:7–8 NLT

Pay careful attention to your own work,
for then you will get the satisfaction of a job well done,
and you won't need to compare yourself to anyone else.
For we are each responsible for our own conduct.

GALATIANS 6:4–5 NLT

Oh, how sweet the light of day, and how wonderful
to live in the sunshine! Even if you live a long time,
don't take a single day for granted.
Take delight in each light-filled hour.

ECCLESIASTES 11:7–8 MSG

Be kindly affectionate to one another...;
not lagging in diligence, fervent in spirit, serving
the Lord; rejoicing in hope, patient in tribulation,
continuing steadfastly in prayer; distributing to
the needs of the saints, given to hospitality.

ROMANS 12:10–13 NKJV

Dear friend, listen well to my words....
Those who discover these words live,
really live; body and soul....
Keep vigilant watch over your heart;
that's where life starts.

PROVERBS 4:20–23 MSG

Eternity

One thing I ask from the LORD,
this only do I seek:
that I may dwell in the house of the LORD
all the days of my life,
to gaze on the beauty of the LORD
and to seek him in his temple.

PSALM 27:4 NIV

For our light and momentary troubles are achieving
for us an eternal glory that far outweighs them all.
So we fix our eyes not on what is seen, but on
what is unseen. For what is seen is temporary,
but what is unseen is eternal.

2 CORINTHIANS 4:17–18 NIV

Before the mountains were brought forth,
or ever you had formed the earth and the world,
from everlasting to everlasting you are God.

PSALM 90:2 NRSV

We are citizens of heaven, where the Lord Jesus Christ
lives. And we are eagerly waiting for him to return as our
Savior. He will take our weak mortal bodies and change
them into glorious bodies like his own.

PHILIPPIANS 3:20–21 NLT

Surely goodness and mercy shall follow me
All the days of my life;
And I will dwell in the house of the LORD
Forever.

PSALM 23:6 NKJV

Faith

Now faith is the assurance of things hoped for,
the conviction of things not seen.

Hebrews 11:1 nasb

Let your roots grow down into him, and let your lives be
built on him. Then your faith will grow strong in the truth
you were taught, and you will overflow with thankfulness.

Colossians 2:7 nlt

Without faith it is impossible to please God, because
anyone who comes to him must believe that he exists and
that he rewards those who earnestly seek him.

Hebrews 11:6 niv

For we walk by faith, not by sight.

2 Corinthians 5:7 nkjv

The Good News shows how God makes
people right with himself—that it begins
and ends with faith. As the Scripture says,
"But those who are right with God will live by faith."

Romans 1:17 ncv

Be on your guard; stand firm in the faith;
be courageous; be strong.

1 Corinthians 16:13 niv

God's love, though, is ever and always,
eternally present to all who fear him,
making everything right for them
and their children as they follow
his Covenant ways.

Psalm 103:17–18 msg

Faithfulness

God is faithful. He will not allow the temptation to be more than you can stand. When you are tempted, he will show you a way out so that you can endure.

1 CORINTHIANS 10:13 NLT

Your love, Lord, reaches to the heavens,
your faithfulness to the skies....
How priceless is your unfailing love, O God!
People take refuge in the shadow of your wings.
They feast on the abundance of your house;
you give them drink from your river of delights.
For with you is the fountain of life;
in your light we see light.

PSALM 36:5, 7-9 NIV

The Lord is faithful, and he will
strengthen you and protect you.

2 THESSALONIANS 3:3 NIV

The steadfast love of the LORD never ceases,
his mercies never come to an end;
they are new every morning;
great is your faithfulness.

LAMENTATIONS 3:22–23 NRSV

I will sing of the LORD's great love forever;
with my mouth I will make your faithfulness known
through all generations.
I will declare that your love stands firm forever,
that you have established your faithfulness in heaven itself.

PSALM 89:1–2 NIV

Family

Be kindly affectionate to one another with brotherly love,
in honor giving preference to one another.

ROMANS 12:10 NKJV

You're blessed when you can show people
how to cooperate instead of compete or fight.
That's when you discover who you really are,
and your place in God's family.

MATTHEW 5:9 MSG

All of you, be like-minded,
be sympathetic, love one another,
be compassionate and humble.

1 PETER 3:8 NIV

Brothers and sisters, we ask you to appreciate those who work hard among you, who lead you in the Lord and teach you. Respect them with a very special love because of the work they do. Live in peace with each other.... Be patient with everyone. Be sure that no one pays back wrong for wrong, but always try to do what is good for each other and for all people.

1 THESSALONIANS 5:12–15 NCV

Make the most of every opportunity. Be gracious in your speech. The goal is to bring out the best in others.

COLOSSIANS 4:5–6 MSG

As for me and my household, we will serve the LORD.

JOSHUA 24:15 NIV

Fear

God has not given us a spirit of fear and timidity,
but of power, love, and self-discipline.

2 Timothy 1:7 nlt

Where God's love is, there is no fear, because God's perfect
love drives out fear. It is punishment that makes a person
fear, so love is not made perfect in the person who fears.

1 John 4:18 ncv

You did not receive a spirit of slavery to fall back into fear,
but you have received a spirit of adoption. When we cry,
"Abba! Father!" it is that very Spirit bearing witness with
our spirit that we are children of God.

Romans 8:15–16 nrsv

Even though I walk through the valley of the shadow of death,
I fear no evil, for You are with me;
Your rod and Your staff, they comfort me.
You prepare a table before me in the presence of my enemies;
You have anointed my head with oil;
My cup overflows.

PSALM 23:4–5 NASB

Have no fear of sudden disaster
or of the ruin that overtakes the wicked,
for the LORD will be at your side
and will keep your foot from being snared.

PROVERBS 3:25–26 NIV

Finances

Wealth from get-rich-quick schemes quickly disappears;
wealth from hard work grows over time.

Proverbs 13:11 NLT

The Lord makes firm the steps
of the one who delights in him;
though he may stumble, he will not fall,
for the Lord upholds him with his hand.
I was young and now I am old,
yet I have never seen the righteous forsaken
or their children begging bread.

Psalm 37:23–25 NIV

Teach those who are rich in this world not to be proud and not to trust in their money, which is so unreliable. Their trust should be in God, who richly gives us all we need for our enjoyment. Tell them to use their money to do good. They should be rich in good works and generous to those in need, always being ready to share with others. By doing this they will be storing up their treasure as a good foundation for the future so that they may experience true life.

1 TIMOTHY 6:17–19 NLT

My God shall supply all your needs according to His riches in glory by Christ Jesus.

PHILIPPIANS 4:19 NKJV

Flexibility

Let your conversation be always full of grace,
seasoned with salt, so that you may know
how to answer everyone.

Colossians 4:6 niv

Accept other believers...and don't argue with them about
what they think is right or wrong. For instance...those who
worship the Lord on a special day do it to honor him.
Those who eat any kind of food do so to honor the Lord,
since they give thanks to God before eating. And those
who refuse to eat certain foods also want to please
the Lord and give thanks to God.

Romans 14:1–2, 6 nlt

I prefer a flexible heart to an inflexible ritual.

MATTHEW 12:7 MSG

You are our Father;

We are the clay, and You our potter;

And all we are the work of Your hand.

ISAIAH 64:8 NKJV

It's not important who does the planting, or who does the watering. What's important is that God makes the seed grow. The one who plants and the one who waters work together with the same purpose. And both will be rewarded for their own hard work.

1 CORINTHIANS 3:7–8 NLT

Forgiveness

The LORD is compassionate and gracious,
slow to anger, abounding in love.
He will not always accuse,
nor will he harbor his anger forever;
he does not treat us as our sins deserve
or repay us according to our iniquities.
For as high as the heavens are above the earth,
so great is his love for those who fear him;
as far as the east is from the west,
so far has he removed our transgressions from us.

PSALM 103:8–12 NIV

If anyone is in Christ, he is a new creation;
old things have passed away; behold,
all things have become new.

2 CORINTHIANS 5:17 NKJV

If we confess our sins, He is faithful and just to forgive us
our sins and to cleanse us from all unrighteousness.

1 JOHN 1:9 NKJV

Make allowance for each other's faults, and forgive
anyone who offends you. Remember, the Lord forgave you,
so you must forgive others.

COLOSSIANS 3:13 NLT

Whenever you stand praying, forgive, if you have
anything against anyone; so that your Father in heaven
may also forgive you.

MARK 11:25 NRSV

If you forgive other people when they sin against you,
your heavenly Father will also forgive you.

MATTHEW 6:14 NIV

Friendship

Do to others whatever you would like them to do to you.
This is the essence of all that is taught
in the law and the prophets.

MATTHEW 7:12 NLT

The right word at the right time
is like a custom-made piece of jewelry,
And a wise friend's timely reprimand
is like a gold ring slipped on your finger.
Reliable friends who do what they say
are like cool drinks in sweltering heat—refreshing!

PROVERBS 25:12–13 MSG

Two are better than one,
because they have a good return for their labor:
If either of them falls down,
one can help the other up.

ECCLESIASTES 4:9–10 NIV

There are "friends" who pretend to be friends,
but there is a friend who sticks closer than a brother.

PROVERBS 18:24 TLB

A friend loves at all times.

PROVERBS 17:17 NKJV

This is my commandment, that you love one another as I
have loved you. No one has greater love than this,
to lay down one's life for one's friends.

JOHN 15:12–13 NRSV

The amazing grace of the Master, Jesus Christ,
the extravagant love of God, the intimate friendship of the
Holy Spirit, be with all of you.

2 CORINTHIANS 13:14 MSG

Generosity

Remember this—a farmer who plants only
a few seeds will get a small crop. But the one
who plants generously will get a generous crop.
You must each decide in your heart how much to give.
And don't give reluctantly or in response to pressure.
"For God loves a person who gives cheerfully."
And God will generously provide all you need.
Then you will always have everything you need
and plenty left over to share with others....
Yes, you will be enriched in every way so that you can
always be generous. And when we take your gifts
to those who need them, they will thank God.

2 CORINTHIANS 9:6–8, 11 NLT

You know how to give good gifts to your children.
How much more your heavenly Father will give
good things to those who ask him!

Matthew 7:11 ncv

A generous person will prosper;
whoever refreshes others will be refreshed.

Proverbs 11:25 niv

Give, and it will be given to you. A good measure,
pressed down, shaken together and running over,
will be poured into your lap. For with the measure you use,
it will be measured to you.

Luke 6:38 niv

Goodness

Let us not become weary in doing good, for at the proper time we will reap a harvest if we do not give up. Therefore, as we have opportunity, let us do good to all people.

GALATIANS 6:9–10 NIV

He has told you, O man, what is good;
And what does the LORD require of you
But to do justice, to love kindness,
And to walk humbly with your God?

MICAH 6:8 NASB

Always pursue what is good both for yourselves and for all. Rejoice always, pray without ceasing, in everything give thanks.... Test all things; hold fast what is good.

1 THESSALONIANS 5:15–18, 21 NKJV

Keep your eyes focused on what is right,
and look straight ahead to what is good.

PROVERBS 4:25 NCV

Taste and see that the LORD is good;
blessed is the one who takes refuge in him.

PSALM 34:8 NIV

Make sure you don't take things for granted and
go slack in working for the common good; share
what you have with others. God takes particular pleasure
in acts of worship…that take place in kitchen
and workplace and on the streets.

HEBREWS 13:16 MSG

Grace

We are made right with God by placing our faith in Jesus Christ. And this is true for everyone who believes, no matter who we are. For everyone has sinned; we all fall short of God's glorious standard. Yet God, with undeserved kindness, declares that we are righteous. He did this through Christ Jesus when he freed us from the penalty for our sins.

ROMANS 3:22–24 NLT

For the LORD God is our sun and our shield.
He gives us grace and glory.
The LORD will withhold no good thing
from those who do what is right.

PSALM 84:11 NLT

Sin didn't, and doesn't, have a chance in competition
with the aggressive forgiveness we call *grace*. When it's sin
versus grace, grace wins hands down. All sin can do is
threaten us with death.... Grace...invites us into life—a life
that goes on and on and on, world without end.

ROMANS 5:20–21 MSG

He has saved us and called us to a holy life—
not because of anything we have done but
because of his own purpose and grace.

2 TIMOTHY 1:9 NIV

My grace is sufficient for you, for My strength
is made perfect in weakness.

2 CORINTHIANS 12:9 NKJV

Grief

May our Lord Jesus Christ himself and God our Father,
who loved us and through grace gave us eternal comfort
and good hope, comfort your hearts and
strengthen them in every good work and word.

2 THESSALONIANS 2:16–17 NRSV

Jesus said to her, "I am the resurrection and the life. He
who believes in Me, though he may die, he shall live."

JOHN 11:25 NKJV

He will wipe every tear from their eyes, and there will be
no more death or sorrow or crying or pain.
All these things are gone forever.

REVELATION 21:4 NLT

It has now been revealed through the appearing of our
Savior Christ Jesus, who abolished death and brought life
and immortality to light through the gospel.

2 TIMOTHY 1:10 NRSV

You're blessed when you feel you've lost
what is most dear to you. Only then can you be embraced
by the One most dear to you.

MATTHEW 5:4 MSG

Praise be to the God and Father of our Lord Jesus Christ,
the Father of compassion and the God of all comfort,
who comforts us in all our troubles.

2 CORINTHIANS 1:3–4 NIV

Guidance

Trust in the L<small>ORD</small> with all your heart,
And lean not on your own understanding;
In all your ways acknowledge Him,
And He shall direct your paths.

P<small>ROVERBS</small> 3:5–6 <small>NKJV</small>

When we obey him, every path he guides us on is fragrant
with his lovingkindness and his truth.

P<small>SALM</small> 25:10 <small>TLB</small>

I'll take the hand of those who don't know the way,
who can't see where they're going.
I'll be a personal guide to them,
directing them through unknown country.

I<small>SAIAH</small> 42:16 <small>MSG</small>

The Lord directs the steps of the godly.
He delights in every detail of their lives.
Though they stumble, they will never fall,
for the Lord holds them by the hand.

Psalm 37:23–24 NLT

I will instruct you and teach you in the way you should go;
I will counsel you with my loving eye on you.

Psalm 32:8 NIV

When you turn to the right or when you turn to the left,
your ears shall hear a word behind you, saying,
"This is the way; walk in it."

Isaiah 30:21 NRSV

Guilt

Therefore, there is now no condemnation for those
who are in Christ Jesus, because through Christ Jesus
the law of the Spirit who gives life has set you free
from the law of sin and death.

ROMANS 8:1–2 NIV

Whoever hears my word and believes him who
sent me has eternal life and will not be judged
but has crossed over from death to life.

JOHN 5:24 NIV

I, I am the One who erases all your sins, for my sake;
I will not remember your sins.

ISAIAH 43:25 NCV

Dear brothers and sisters, we can boldly enter heaven's
Most Holy Place because of the blood of Jesus. By his
death, Jesus opened a new and life-giving way through the
curtain into the Most Holy Place. And since we have a great
High Priest who rules over God's house, let us go right into
the presence of God with sincere hearts fully trusting him.

HEBREWS 10:19–22 NLT

God did not send his Son into the world to condemn
the world, but to save the world through him.
Whoever believes in him is not condemned.

JOHN 3:17–18 NIV

Health

Praise the LORD, my soul,
and forget not all his benefits—
who forgives all your sins
and heals all your diseases,
who redeems your life from the pit
and crowns you with love and compassion,
who satisfies your desires with good things
so that your youth is renewed like the eagle's.

PSALM 103:2–5 NIV

Beloved, I pray that all may go well with you and that you
may be in good health, just as it is well with your soul.

3 JOHN 1:2 NRSV

A cheerful heart is good medicine.

PROVERBS 17:22 NIV

Are you hurting? Pray. Do you feel great? Sing.
Are you sick? Call the church leaders together to pray
and anoint you with oil in the name of the Master.
Believing-prayer will heal you, and Jesus will
put you on your feet. And if you've sinned,
you'll be forgiven—healed inside and out.

JAMES 5:14–15 MSG

My child, pay attention to what I say.
Listen carefully to my words.
Don't lose sight of them.
Let them penetrate deep into your heart,
for they bring life to those who find them,
and healing to their whole body.

PROVERBS 4:20–22 NLT

Helpfulness

Carry each other's burdens, and in this way you will fulfill
the law of Christ.... Therefore, as we have opportunity,
let us do good to all people.

GALATIANS 6:2, 10 NIV

God is not unjust; he will not forget your work and the love
you have shown him as you have helped his people
and continue to help them.

HEBREWS 6:10 NIV

Are your hearts tender and compassionate?
Then make me truly happy by agreeing wholeheartedly
with each other, loving one another, and working together
with one mind and purpose.

PHILIPPIANS 2:1–2 NLT

"Lord, when was it that we saw you hungry and gave you food, or thirsty and gave you something to drink? And when was it that we saw you a stranger and welcomed you, or naked and gave you clothing? And when was it that we saw you sick or in prison and visited you?" And the king will answer them, "Truly I tell you, just as you did it to one of the least of these who are members of my family, you did it to me."

MATTHEW 25:37–40 NRSV

Do not forget to show hospitality to strangers, for by so doing some people have shown hospitality to angels without knowing it.

HEBREWS 13:2 NIV

Heritage

These commandments that I give you today are to be on
your hearts. Impress them on your children.
Talk about them when you sit at home and when you walk
along the road, when you lie down and when you get up.
Tie them as symbols on your hands and bind them
on your foreheads. Write them on the doorframes of your
houses and on your gates.

DEUTERONOMY 6:6–9 NIV

I will sing of the mercies of the LORD forever;
With my mouth will I make known
Your faithfulness to all generations.

PSALM 89:1 NKJV

Children are a heritage from the LORD,
offspring a reward from him.

PSALM 127:3 NIV

Let the message of Christ dwell among you richly as you teach and admonish one another with all wisdom through psalms, hymns, and songs from the Spirit, singing to God with gratitude in your hearts.

Colossians 3:16 niv

Commit yourselves wholeheartedly to these words of mine. Tie them to your hands and wear them on your forehead as reminders. Teach them to your children. Talk about them when you are at home and when you are on the road, when you are going to bed and when you are getting up.

Deuteronomy 11:18–19 nlt

Hope

O Lord, you alone are my hope
I've trusted you, O Lord, from childhood.
Yes, you have been with me from birth;
from my mother's womb you have cared for me.
No wonder I am always praising you!
My life is an example to many,
because you have been my strength and protection.
That is why I can never stop praising you;
I declare your glory all day long.

PSALM 71:5–8 NLT

The Lord is good to those whose hope is in him,
to the one who seeks him.

LAMENTATIONS 3:25 NIV

Blessed be the God and Father of our Lord Jesus Christ!
By his great mercy he has given us a new birth into a living
hope through the resurrection of Jesus Christ.

1 Peter 1:3 nrsv

God...rekindles burned-out lives with fresh hope,
Restoring dignity and respect to their lives—
a place in the sun!

1 Samuel 2:7–8 msg

May the God of hope fill you with all joy and peace as you
trust in him, so that you may overflow with hope by the
power of the Holy Spirit.

Romans 15:13 niv

94

Inspiration

You are the light of the world. A city built on a hill cannot be hid. No one after lighting a lamp puts it under the bushel basket, but on the lampstand, and it gives light to all in the house. In the same way, let your light shine before others, so that they may see your good works and give glory to your Father in heaven.

MATTHEW 5:14–16 NRSV

Take your everyday, ordinary life—your sleeping, eating, going-to-work, and walking-around life—and place it before God as an offering. Embracing what God does for you is the best thing you can do for him.

ROMANS 12:1 MSG

I am the Light of the world; he who follows Me will not walk in the darkness, but will have the Light of life.

JOHN 8:12 NASB

Since we are surrounded by such a huge crowd of witnesses to the life of faith, let us strip off every weight that slows us down.... And let us run with endurance the race God has set before us.

HEBREWS 12:1 NLT

To him who is able to do immeasurably more than all we ask or imagine, according to his power that is at work within us, to him be glory.

EPHESIANS 3:20–21 NIV

Joy

This is the day the L ORD has made;
We will rejoice and be glad in it.

PSALM 118:24 NKJV

Be truly glad! There is wonderful joy ahead....
You love him even though you have never seen him.
Though you do not see him now, you trust him; and you
rejoice with a glorious, inexpressible joy.

1 PETER 1:6, 8 NLT

You make known to me the path of life;
you will fill me with joy in your presence,
with eternal pleasures at your right hand.

PSALM 16:11 NIV

Why is everyone hungry for more?
"More, more," they say. "More, more."
I have God's more-than-enough,
More joy in one ordinary day
Than they get in all their shopping sprees.
At day's end I'm ready for sound sleep,
For you, GOD, have put my life back together.

PSALM 4:6–8 MSG

A cheerful look brings joy to the heart;
good news makes for good health.

PROVERBS 15:30 NLT

Happy are those who hear the joyful call to worship,
for they will walk in the light of your presence, LORD.

PSALM 89:15 NLT

Justice

Learn to do right; seek justice.
Defend the oppressed.
Take up the cause of the fatherless;
plead the case of the widow.

ISAIAH 1:17 NIV

To do what is right and just
is more acceptable to the LORD than sacrifice.

PROVERBS 21:3 NIV

He will not judge by appearance, false evidence,
or hearsay, but will defend the poor and the exploited.
He will rule against the wicked who oppress them. For he
will be clothed with fairness and with truth.

ISAIAH 11:3–5 TLB

His work is perfect,
For all His ways are just;
A God of faithfulness and without injustice,
Righteous and upright is He.

DEUTERONOMY 32:4 NASB

The LORD secures justice for the poor
and upholds the cause of the needy.

PSALM 140:12 NIV

Beloved, do not avenge yourselves, but rather
give place to wrath; for it is written, "Vengeance is Mine,
I will repay," says the Lord.

ROMANS 12:19 NKJV

Kindness

For His merciful kindness is great toward us,
And the truth of the Lord endures forever.
Praise the Lord!

PSALM 117:2 NKJV

Blessed be the Lord,
For He has shown me His marvelous kindness.

PSALM 31:21 NKJV

Love your enemies, do good to them, and lend to them
without expecting to get anything back. Then your reward
will be great, and you will be children of the Most High.

LUKE 6:35 NIV

Be kind and compassionate to one another.

EPHESIANS 4:32 NIV

I will tell of the kindnesses of the LORD,
the deeds for which he is to be praised,
according to all the LORD has done for us...
according to his compassion and many kindnesses.

ISAIAH 63:7 NIV

If anyone has material possessions and sees a brother or
sister in need but has no pity on them, how can the love of
God be in that person? Dear children, let us not love with
words or speech but with actions and in truth.

1 JOHN 3:17–18 NIV

When she speaks, her words are wise,
and she gives instructions with kindness.

PROVERBS 31:26 NLT

Loneliness

I am convinced that nothing can ever separate us from
God's love. Neither death nor life, neither angels nor
demons, neither our fears for today nor our worries about
tomorrow—not even the powers of hell can separate us
from God's love. No power in the sky above or in the earth
below—indeed, nothing in all creation will ever be able to
separate us from the love of God.

ROMANS 8:38–39 NLT

The LORD is near to all who call on him,
to all who call on him in truth.

PSALM 145:18 NIV

Remember, I am with you always, to the end of the age.

MATTHEW 28:20 NRSV

By this we know that we abide in Him and He in us,

because He has given us of His Spirit.

1 JOHN 4:13 NASB

O LORD, You have searched me and known me.

You know my sitting down and my rising up;

You understand my thought afar off.

You comprehend my path and my lying down,

And are acquainted with all my ways.

For there is not a word on my tongue,

But behold, O LORD, You know it altogether.

PSALM 139:1–4 NKJV

Love

If I speak in the tongues of men or of angels,
but do not have love, I am only a resounding gong
or a clanging cymbal. If I have the gift of prophecy
and can fathom all mysteries and all knowledge,
and if I have a faith that can move mountains,
but do not have love, I am nothing. If I give all I possess
to the poor...but do not have love, I gain nothing.
Love is patient, love is kind. It does not envy, it does not
boast, it is not proud. It does not dishonor others,
it is not self-seeking, it is not easily angered,
it keeps no record of wrongs. Love does not delight in
evil but rejoices with the truth. It always protects,
always trusts, always hopes, always perseveres.
Love never fails.

1 Corinthians 13:1–8 niv

What great love the Father has lavished on us,
that we should be called children of God!
And that is what we are!

1 JOHN 3:1 NIV

This is how much God loved the world:
He gave his Son, his one and only Son.
And this is why: so that no one need be destroyed;
by believing in him, anyone can have
a whole and lasting life.

JOHN 3:16 MSG

Patience

As those who have been chosen of God, holy and beloved,
put on a heart of compassion, kindness, humility,
gentleness and patience.... Beyond all these things
put on love, which is the perfect bond of unity.

COLOSSIANS 3:12, 14 NASB

Always be prepared to give an answer to everyone
who asks you to give the reason for the hope that you have.
But do this with gentleness and respect.

1 PETER 3:15 NIV

Be like those who through faith and patience
will receive what God has promised.

HEBREWS 6:12 NCV

God is pleased with you when you do what you know is
right and patiently endure unfair treatment.

1 PETER 2:19 NLT

All of you be harmonious, sympathetic, brotherly,
kindhearted, and humble in spirit; not returning evil for
evil or insult for insult, but giving a blessing instead;
for you were called for the very purpose that you might
inherit a blessing.

1 PETER 3:8–9 NASB

May the Lord lead your hearts into a full understanding
and expression of the love of God and the patient
endurance that comes from Christ.

2 THESSALONIANS 3:5 NLT

Peace

Do not be anxious about anything, but in every situation, by prayer and petition, with thanksgiving, present your requests to God. And the peace of God, which transcends all understanding, will guard your hearts and your minds in Christ Jesus.

PHILIPPIANS 4:6–7 NIV

I am leaving you with a gift—peace of mind and heart! And the peace I give isn't fragile like the peace the world gives. So don't be troubled or afraid.

JOHN 14:27 TLB

These things I have spoken to you, so that in Me you may have peace. In the world you have tribulation, but take courage; I have overcome the world.

JOHN 16:33 NASB

If people's thinking is controlled by the sinful self, there is death. But if their thinking is controlled by the Spirit, there is life and peace.

ROMANS 8:6 NCV

Those who love your instructions have great peace and do not stumble.

PSALM 119:165 NLT

May the Lord of peace himself give you peace at all times and in every way. The Lord be with all of you.

2 THESSALONIANS 3:16 NIV

God is not a God of confusion but of peace.

1 CORINTHIANS 14:33 NASB

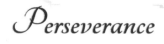

Perseverance

Dear brothers and sisters, I have not achieved it,
but I focus on this one thing: Forgetting the
past and looking forward to what lies ahead,
I press on to reach the end of the race and
receive the heavenly prize for which God,
through Christ Jesus, is calling us.

PHILIPPIANS 3:13–14 NLT

Consider it pure joy…whenever you face trials
of many kinds, because you know that
the testing of your faith develops perseverance.
Perseverance must finish its work so that
you may be mature and complete,
not lacking anything.

JAMES 1:2–4 NIV

Let us not grow weary of doing what is right, for we will reap at harvest time, if we do not give up.

GALATIANS 6:9 NRSV

I waited patiently for the LORD;
he turned to me and heard my cry.
He lifted me out of the slimy pit,
out of the mud and mire;
he set my feet on a rock
and gave me a firm place to stand.
He put a new song in my mouth,
a hymn of praise to our God.
Many will see and fear the LORD
and put their trust in him.

PSALM 40:1–3 NIV

Praise

By Him let us continually offer the sacrifice
of praise to God, that is, the fruit of our lips,
giving thanks to His name.

HEBREWS 13:15 NKJV

Praise the LORD from the heavens;
praise him in the heights above.
Praise him, all his angels;
praise him, all his heavenly hosts.
Praise him, sun and moon;
praise him, all you shining stars.
Praise him, you highest heavens
and you waters above the skies.
Let them praise the name of the LORD,
for at his command they were created.

PSALM 148:1–5 NIV

O LORD, You are my God.
I will exalt You,
I will praise Your name,
For You have done wonderful things.

ISAIAH 25:1 NKJV

A time is coming and has now come when the true
worshipers will worship the Father in the Spirit and in
truth, for they are the kind of worshipers the Father seeks.
God is spirit, and his worshipers must worship
in the Spirit and in truth.

JOHN 4:23–24 NIV

Sing praises to the LORD,
you his faithful people;
praise his holy name.

PSALM 30:4 NIV

Prayer

Don't worry about anything; instead, pray about
everything. Tell God what you need, and thank him
for all he has done.

PHILIPPIANS 4:6 NLT

I call on you, my God, for you will answer me;
turn your ear to me and hear my prayer.
Show me the wonders of your great love.

PSALM 17:6–7 NIV

I prayed to the LORD, and he answered me.
He freed me from all my fears.
Those who look to him for help will be radiant with joy.

PSALM 34:4–5 NLT

The Spirit also helps our weakness; for we do not know how to pray as we should, but the Spirit Himself intercedes for us with groanings too deep for words.

ROMANS 8:26 NASB

You, God, are my God, earnestly I seek you; I thirst for you, my whole being longs for you, in a dry and parched land where there is no water.

PSALM 63:1 NIV

My voice You shall hear in the morning, O LORD;
In the morning I will direct it to You,
And I will look up.

PSALM 5:3 NKJV

Promises

Not one word of all the good words which the Lord
your God spoke concerning you has failed;
all have been fulfilled for you.

JOSHUA 23:14 NASB

You will show us your faithfulness
and unfailing love as you promised.

MICAH 7:20 NLT

You believe in God, believe also in Me.
In My Father's house are many mansions.
I go to prepare a place for you.
And if I go and prepare a place for you,
I will come again and receive you to Myself;
that where I am, you may be also.

JOHN 14:1–3 NKJV

He has granted to us His precious and
magnificent promises, so that by them you may become
partakers of the divine nature, having escaped
the corruption that is in the world.

2 PETER 1:4 NASB

I have thoroughly tested your promises,
and that is why I love them so much.

PSALM 119:140 TLB

The LORD is trustworthy in all he promises
and faithful in all he does.

PSALM 145:13 NIV

For all of God's promises have been fulfilled
in Christ with a resounding "Yes!"

2 CORINTHIANS 1:20 NLT

Provision

God is able to bless you abundantly, so that in all things
at all times, having all that you need, you will abound in
every good work.... You will be enriched in every way so
that you can be generous on every occasion, and through
us your generosity will result in thanksgiving to God.
This service that you perform is not only supplying the
needs of the Lord's people but is also overflowing
in many expressions of thanks to God.

2 Corinthians 9:8, 11–12 niv

Seek first the kingdom of God and His righteousness,
and all these things shall be added to you. Therefore
do not worry about tomorrow, for tomorrow
will worry about its own things.

Matthew 6:33–34 nkjv

You care for the land and water it;
you enrich it abundantly. The streams of God are
filled with water to provide the people with grain,
for so you have ordained it.

PSALM 65:9 NIV

You can be sure that God will take care of
everything you need, his generosity exceeding
even yours in the glory that pours from Jesus.
Our God and Father abounds in glory
that just pours out into eternity.

PHILIPPIANS 4:19–20 MSG

Purpose

You make known to me the path of life;
you will fill me with joy in your presence.

PSALM 16:11 NIV

What happens when we live God's way? He brings
gifts into our lives...things like affection for others,
exuberance about life..., a sense of compassion in the heart,
and a conviction that a basic holiness
permeates things and people.

GALATIANS 5:22–23 MSG

We know that all things work together for good
to those who love God, to those who are the called
according to His purpose.

ROMANS 8:28 NKJV

Live as citizens of heaven, conducting yourselves in a
manner worthy of the Good News about Christ...
standing together with one spirit and one purpose,
fighting together for the faith. Don't be intimidated in any
way by your enemies. This will be a sign to them that you
are going to be saved, even by God himself.

PHILIPPIANS 1:27–28 NLT

Be attentive to my words;
incline your ear to my sayings.
Do not let them escape from your sight;
keep them within your heart....
Let your eyes look directly forward,
and your gaze be straight before you.

PROVERBS 4:20–21, 25 NRSV

Relationships

As those who have been chosen of God,
holy and beloved, put on a heart of compassion,
kindness, humility, gentleness and patience;
bearing with one another, and forgiving each
other, whoever has a complaint against anyone;
just as the Lord forgave you, so also should you.
Beyond all these things put on love,
which is the perfect bond of unity.

COLOSSIANS 3:12–14 NASB

Perfume and incense bring joy to the heart,
and the pleasantness of a friend
springs from their heartfelt advice.

PROVERBS 27:9 NIV

Love each other with genuine affection,
and take delight in honoring each other.

ROMANS 12:10 NLT

Two are better than one,
because they have a good return for their labor:
If either of them falls down,
one can help the other up.

ECCLESIASTES 4:9–10 NIV

Seek to do good to one another and to all.

1 THESSALONIANS 5:15 NRSV

Let us consider how we may spur one another on
toward love and good deeds.

HEBREWS 10:24–25 NIV

Reliability

The grass withers,
And its flower falls away,
But the word of the Lord endures forever.

1 Peter 1:24–25 nkjv

The things you have heard me say in the presence
of many witnesses entrust to reliable people who will also
be qualified to teach others.

2 Timothy 2:2 niv

He will give eternal life to those who keep on doing good,
seeking after the glory and honor
and immortality that God offers.

Romans 2:7 nlt

Jesus Christ is the same yesterday and today and forever.

Hebrews 13:8 nasb

2

With all my heart I have sought You;
Do not let me wander from Your commandments.
Your word I have treasured in my heart,
That I may not sin against You.
Teach me, O LORD, the way of Your statutes,
And I shall observe it to the end.

PSALM 119:10–11, 33 NASB

Be on your guard, so that you do not lose what we
have worked for, but may receive a full reward.

2 JOHN 1:8 NRSV

You are near, LORD,
and all your commands are true.
Long ago I learned from your statutes
that you established them to last forever.

PSALM 119:151–152 NIV

Salvation

God...has given us new birth into a living hope through
the resurrection of Jesus Christ from the dead, and into an
inheritance that can never perish, spoil or fade.
This inheritance is kept in heaven for you.

1 PETER 1:3–4 NIV

If you declare with your mouth, "Jesus is Lord,"
and believe in your heart that God raised him
from the dead, you will be saved.

ROMANS 10:9 NIV

God so loved the world that he gave his one
and only Son, that whoever believes in him
shall not perish but have eternal life.

JOHN 3:16 NIV

Once you were dead because of your disobedience and your
many sins.... All of us used to live that way, following the
passionate desires and inclinations of our sinful nature.
By our very nature we were subject to God's anger,
just like everyone else. But God is so rich in mercy,
and he loved us so much, that even though
we were dead because of our sins, he gave us life
when he raised Christ from the dead.

Ephesians 2:1, 3–5 NLT

I will praise You,
For You have answered me,
And have become my salvation.

Psalm 118:21 NKJV

Serving

He who is greatest among you, let him be as the younger,
and he who governs as he who serves. For who
is greater, he who sits at the table, or he who serves?
Is it not he who sits at the table?
Yet I am among you as the One who serves.

LUKE 22:26–27 NKJV

Always give yourselves fully to the work of the Lord, because
you know that your labor in the Lord is not in vain.

1 CORINTHIANS 15:58 NIV

We are not saying that we can do this work ourselves.
It is God who makes us able to do all that we do.

2 CORINTHIANS 3:5 NCV

Each of you should use whatever gift
you have received to serve others, as faithful stewards
of God's grace in its various forms.

1 PETER 4:10 NIV

We are God's handiwork, created in Christ Jesus to do
good works, which God prepared in advance for us to do.

EPHESIANS 2:10 NIV

God is not unjust; he will not overlook your work
and the love that you showed for his sake in
serving the saints, as you still do.

HEBREWS 6:10 NRSV

Stress

The LORD also will be a refuge for the oppressed,
A refuge in times of trouble.
And those who know Your name will put their trust in You;
For You, LORD, have not forsaken those who seek You.

PSALM 9:9–10 NKJV

Blessed is the one who trusts in the LORD,
whose confidence is in him.
They will be like a tree planted by the water
that sends out its roots by the stream.
It does not fear when heat comes;
its leaves are always green.
It has no worries in a year of drought
and never fails to bear fruit.

JEREMIAH 17:7–8 NIV

Commit your actions to the LORD,
and your plans will succeed.

PROVERBS 16:3 NLT

You're blessed when you're at the end of your rope.
With less of you there is more of God and his rule.

MATTHEW 5:3 MSG

Be glad for all God is planning for you.
Be patient in trouble, and prayerful always.

ROMANS 12:12 TLB

May the God who gives endurance and encouragement give
you the same attitude of mind toward each other
that Christ Jesus had.

ROMANS 15:5 NIV

Teaching

All scripture is inspired by God and is useful for teaching,
for reproof, for correction, and for training
in righteousness, so that everyone who belongs to God
may be proficient, equipped for every good work.

2 TIMOTHY 3:16–17 NRSV

No discipline seems pleasant at the time, but painful.
Later on, however, it produces a harvest of righteousness
and peace for those who have been trained by it.

HEBREWS 12:11 NIV

Don't you realize that in a race everyone runs, but only one
person gets the prize? So run to win! All athletes are
disciplined in their training. They do it to win a prize that
will fade away, but we do it for an eternal prize.

1 CORINTHIANS 9:24–25 NLT

Let each generation tell its children of your mighty acts;

let them proclaim your power.

PSALM 145:4 NLT

Stories we heard from our fathers,

counsel we learned at our mother's knee.

We're not keeping this to ourselves,

we're passing it along to the next generation—

GOD's fame and fortune,

the marvelous things he has done.

PSALM 78:2–4 MSG

Go therefore and make disciples...teaching them to

observe all things that I have commanded you; and lo,

I am with you always.

MATTHEW 28:19–20 NKJV

Thankfulness

May you be filled with joy, always thanking the Father.
He has enabled you to share in the inheritance that belongs
to his people, who live in the light.

COLOSSIANS 1:11–12 NLT

Give thanks to the LORD, for he is good;
his love endures forever.

1 CHRONICLES 16:34 NIV

Let us come into his presence with thanksgiving;
let us make a joyful noise to him with songs of praise!

PSALM 95:2 NRSV

Let the message about Christ, in all its richness,
fill your lives. Teach and counsel each other with all the
wisdom he gives. Sing psalms and hymns and spiritual
songs to God with thankful hearts.

COLOSSIANS 3:16 NLT

Rejoice always, pray without ceasing, in everything give thanks; for this is the will of God in Christ Jesus for you.

1 THESSALONIANS 5:16–18 NKJV

Enter his gates with thanksgiving,
and his courts with praise.
Give thanks to him, bless his name.
For the LORD is good;
his steadfast love endures forever,
and his faithfulness to all generations.

PSALM 100:4–5 NRSV

I will praise the name of God with song
And magnify Him with thanksgiving.

PSALM 69:30 NASB

Trust

The LORD is my strength and my shield;
my heart trusts in him, and he helps me.

PSALM 28:7 NIV

He established a decree...
which he commanded our ancestors
to teach to their children;
that the next generation might know them,
the children yet unborn,
and rise up and tell them to their children,
so that they should set their hope in God.

PSALM 78:5–7 NRSV

Those who know Your name will put their trust in You;
For You, LORD, have not forsaken those who seek You.

PSALM 9:10 NKJV

Whom have I in heaven but you?
And earth has nothing I desire besides you.
My flesh and my heart may fail,
but God is the strength of my heart
and my portion forever.

PSALM 73:25–26 NIV

May God himself, the God who makes everything
holy and whole, make you holy and whole,
put you together—spirit, soul, and body—
and keep you fit for the coming of our Master,
Jesus Christ. The One who called you
is completely dependable.

1 THESSALONIANS 5:24 MSG

Truth

Listen, for I will speak of excellent things,
And from the opening of my lips will come right things;
For my mouth will speak truth.

PROVERBS 8:6–7 NKJV

Jesus said, "If you hold to my teaching, you are
really my disciples. Then you will know the truth,
and the truth will set you free."

JOHN 8:31–32 NIV

Teach me your ways, O LORD,
that I may live according to your truth!
Grant me purity of heart,
so that I may honor you.

PSALM 86:11 NLT

When he, the Spirit of truth, comes,
he will guide you into all the truth.

JOHN 16:13 NIV

Anyone who examines this evidence will come to stake his
life on this: that God himself is the truth.

JOHN 3:33 MSG

Jesus answered, "I am the way and the truth and the life.
No one comes to the Father except through me."

JOHN 14:6 NIV

We will not hide these truths from our children;
we will tell the next generation
about the glorious deeds of the LORD,
about his power and his mighty wonders.

PSALM 78:4 NLT

Wisdom

The Spirit of the LORD will rest on him—
the Spirit of wisdom and understanding....
In that day the wolf and the lamb will live together...
and a little child will lead them all.

ISAIAH 11:2, 6 NLT

The wisdom from above is first pure, then peaceable,
gentle, willing to yield, full of mercy and good fruits,
without a trace of partiality or hypocrisy.

JAMES 3:17 NRSV

If any of you lacks wisdom, you should ask God,
who gives generously to all without finding fault,
and it will be given to you.

JAMES 1:5 NIV

Blessed are those who find wisdom,
those who gain understanding,
for she is more profitable than silver
and yields better returns than gold.
She is more precious than rubies;
nothing you desire can compare with her.

PROVERBS 3:13–15 NIV

Oh, the depth of the riches both of the wisdom
and knowledge of God! How unsearchable are
His judgments and unfathomable His ways!

ROMANS 11:33 NASB

Do not let wisdom and understanding out of your sight,
preserve sound judgment and discretion;
they will be life for you.

PROVERBS 3:21–22 NIV

Worry

Give your burdens to the Lord,
and he will take care of you.

PSALM 55:22 NLT

Do not worry about your life, what you will eat or drink;
or about your body, what you will wear. Is not life
more than food, and the body more than clothes?
Look at the birds of the air; they do not sow or reap or store
away in barns, and yet your heavenly Father feeds them.
Are you not much more valuable than they?

MATTHEW 6:25–26 NIV

Worry weighs a person down;
an encouraging word cheers a person up.

PROVERBS 12:25 NLT

Which of you by worrying can add
a single hour to his life's span?

LUKE 12:25 NASB

Don't worry about anything; instead, pray about
everything. Tell God what you need, and thank him for all
he has done. Then you will experience God's peace,
which exceeds anything we can understand. His peace will
guard your hearts and minds as you live in Christ Jesus.

PHILIPPIANS 4:6–7 NLT

May the Lord of peace himself give you
peace at all times in all ways.

2 THESSALONIANS 3:16 NRSV

Omega

GOD IS THE FINAL ANSWER
FOR ALL THAT WE NEED

Jesus stood and said…"Let anyone who is thirsty
come to me and drink. Whoever believes in me,
as Scripture has said, rivers of living water
will flow from within them."

JOHN 7:37–38 NIV

Jesus…said, "For mortals it is impossible, but not for God;
for God all things are possible."

MARK 10:27 NRSV

He himself is before all things,
and in him all things hold together.

COLOSSIANS 1:17 NRSV

He has made everything beautiful in its time.
He has also set eternity in the human heart;
yet no one can fathom what God has done
from beginning to end.

Ecclesiastes 3:11 NIV

I am the Alpha and the Omega—
the Beginning and the End.
To all who are thirsty I will give freely
from the springs of the water of life.

Revelation 21:6 NLT